TABLE OF CONTENTS

Novel-Ties® are printed on recycled paper.

For the Teacher

This reproducible study guide consists of lessons to use in conjunction with the book *Misty of Chincoteague*. Written in chapter-by-chapter format, the guide contains a synopsis, pre-reading activities, vocabulary and comprehension exercises, as well as extension activities to be used as follow-up to the novel.

In a homogeneous classroom, whole class instruction with one title is appropriate. In a heterogeneous classroom, reading groups should be formed: each group works on a different novel at its reading level. Depending upon the length of time devoted to reading in the classroom, each novel, with its guide and accompanying lessons, may be completed in three to six weeks.

Begin using NOVEL-TIES for guided reading by distributing the novel and a folder to each child. Distribute duplicated pages of the study guide for students to place in their folders. After examining the cover and glancing through the book, students can participate in several pre-reading activities. Vocabulary questions should be considered prior to reading a chapter or group of chapters; all other work should be done after the chapter has been read. Comprehension questions can be answered orally or in writing. The classroom teacher should determine the amount of work to be assigned, always keeping in mind that readers must be nurtured and that the ultimate goal is encouraging students' love of reading.

The benefits of using NOVEL-TIES are numerous. Students read good literature in the original, rather than in abridged or edited form. The good reading habits will be transferred to the books students read independently. Passive readers become active, avid readers.

SYNOPSIS

Assateague Island, off the coast of Virginia, has long been home to bands of wild ponies whose ancestors, according to legend, found refuge there when a Spanish galleon was wrecked offshore. Although Assateague remained a wildlife refuge, the nearby island of Chincoteague was settled. Paul and Maureen Beebe lived on their grandparents' pony farm in Chincoteague. Visiting Assateague one day, the two children resolved to become the owners of the-Phantom, a mysterious mare that had always eluded capture on Pony Penning Day, the traditional annual roundup and horse auction.

To earn money to buy the mare, the children spent four months gentling the wild colts on their grandparents' ranch and doing chores for their neighbors. When Pony Penning Day arrived, Paul was allowed to accompany the adult horsemen to Assateague Island. While the older riders went off to herd the horses to the point of land where they would cross the channel, Paul was sent after a straggler. His resentment at being treated as a child turned to astonishment when he came across the Phantom and her new colt. The Phantom fled toward the cry of her stallion leader, the Pied Piper, who was already at the point. Following close behind, Paul was given credit for bringing in the mare and her colt. As the horsemen drove the wild ponies across the channel to Chincoteague, the Phantom's colt was caught in a whirlpool. Paul plunged into the sea and helped the frail creature swim to safety. Once ashore, the horses were herded down Chincoteague's main street and into pens to be assessed by prospective buyers. Of all the wild ponies, only the Phantom's colt, dubbed Misty, seemed to enjoy the adventure.

The next morning, when the horses were to be sold, Maureen and Paul were disappointed to learn that Misty had already been claimed by an early buyer. A week later, when this buyer won another colt in a raffle, Maureen and Paul became the delighted owners of Misty.

Throughout the following year, the wild mare slowly began to tolerate Maureen and Paul who made friends with Misty. Unlike her mother, the colt immediately took an interest in humans. The children gradually trained the Phantom to accept a rider and began to race her daily. Although she was happy when she ran, the Phantom seemed restless and sad most of the time.

When Pony Penning Day came around again, Paul carried out their plan to enter the Phantom in the evening race, where she beat the reigning champion, Black Comet. The next day, the children took the Phantom to the beach for her daily run. A horse's loud bugle came from the sea, and the Pied Piper, having swum across the channel to retrieve her, rose suddenly from the foam. Instead of driving Phantom back toward the gate and home, Paul let her have her freedom, and the two horses swam the channel back to Assateague. Misty, now old enough to fend for herself, was left behind. It was clear to Paul and Maureen that Misty belonged to her human family and to Chincoteague as surely as her mother belonged to the island of wild things.

BACKGROUND INFORMATION

The Ponies of Assateague

Today, many historians believe that the bands of wild ponies who inhabit Assateague Island are descendants of horses that were turned loose by English colonists in the 1600s; others maintain, however, that the horses came from a Spanish ship carrying supplies to colonists moving north from settlements in Florida and the Caribbean. They support this argument by pointing out that the horses of Assateague are descended from a breed the Spanish favored, a mixture of the native Spanish stock with the Barbary horses ridden by the Moors of North Africa. These ponies were descendants of the desert horses of Arabia and were known for their stamina and ability to endure hunger and thirst. For many decades, the Chincoteague Volunteer Fire Company, the official guardians of the Assateague ponies, have served as volunteers to bring hay to the island and chop open frozen waterholes during severe winters.

Chincoteague Wildlife Refuge

Since 1943, the lower third of Assateague Island off the coast of southeast Maryland has been a national wildlife refuge. It provides sanctuary for more than three hundred species of birds, including egrets, swans, ducks, and geese. Also sharing the island with the wild horses are a variety of small mammals, rabbits, native deer, and several exotic Japanese deer who were released there in 1923. Because the island cannot support unlimited numbers of animals, the horse population seldom grows beyond three hundred. Many people feel that if some colts were not weeded out and sold once a year, the horses would eventually starve.

Pony Penny Day

Since 1924, the Chincoteague Volunteer Fire Company has held the annual Fireman's Carnival and Auction on the last Wednesday and Thursday of July. The island ponies are rounded up and driven across Assateague Channel at low tide. Because the horses are strong swimmers, the crossing is not dangerous. About forty young colts and fillies are sold at the next day's auction, and the money is used to buy winter food for the horses and equipment for the fire department. After the auction, the remaining horses are herded back to the channel and allowed to swim home.

ABOUT THE AUTHOR

Marguerite Henry is best known for her many books about horses, several of which have won prizes for children's literature. In 1949, she was awarded the Newbery medal for *King of the Wind*, based on the true story of a stallion who started out as a cart horse and ended up siring some of the greatest English racehorses.

To write *Misty of Chincoteague*, Ms. Henry visited Chincoteague and attended Pony Penning Day. There, she and her illustrator Wesley Dennis met many of the townspeople and the Beebe family who owned a pony ranch. Later, she used them as characters in the book. On Pony Penning Day she was captivated by the tiny foal Misty, who was to appear in several books. Ms. Henry took Misty back to her Illinois home to live for several years before the mare was finally returned to the Beebe ranch to be bred. Through Ms. Henry's books, the real Misty became a celebrity and even a movie star.

GLOSSARY

bay	horse with a reddish-brown body and black mane and tail
bit and bridle	horse's headgear: bit – metal piece that goes between its teeth; bridle – straps that go around the horse's nose and reins
chestnut	reddish-brown horse
colt	young horse six months or older; often a term used only for male horses
corral	pen for horses and other large animals
dam	mother horse
filly	young female horse more than six months old
foal	*v.* – give birth to a horse; *n.* – horse less than six months old
forelock	hair that grows above a horse's forehead
gentle	tame a horse for riding or work
girth	strap that goes around a horse, used to fasten something to its back
mane	long hair on top of a horse's head and along its neck
manger	box for a horse's food
mare	female horse four years or older
mount	animal used for riding
muzzle	area around a horse's nose
nicker	gentle neigh
pony	any small breed of horse
sorrel	dark reddish-brown or bright chestnut horse with a white mane and tail
stallion	male horse four years or older
suckling	baby horse that is not yet weaned
whicker	low, soft neigh of a horse
whinny	low, gentle neigh of a horse
withers	highest part of a horse's back where its shoulders meet
yearling	horse or other animal in the second year of its life

PRE-READING QUESTIONS AND ACTIVITIES

1. Preview the book by reading the title and author's name and by looking at the illustration on the cover. What do you think the book will be about? Have you read any other books on the same topic or by Marguerite Henry, the author of *Misty of Chincoteague*?

2. Create a K-W-L chart, such as the one below, to brainstorm with your classmates what they know about caring for horses. Fill in columns one and two. Return to the chart after you finish the book to complete column three.

What I Know — K —	What I Want to Know — W —	What I Learned — L —

3. Read the Background Information on the ponies of Assateague on page two of this study guide. Then read the first two pages of *Misty of Chincoteague* to learn which theory about the origin of the horses the author accepted.

4. **Social Studies Connection:** Locate the Middle Atlantic states on a map of the United States. Notice the barrier islands off the coasts of New York, New Jersey, Maryland, and the Carolinas. Then look at the map showing Chincoteague and Assateague Islands at the end of the book. Read the caption which is a description of the geography and inhabitants of the islands. You may consult an encyclopedia to learn more about these islands.

5. Which wildlife refuge is nearest your community? Visit it or read about it at your community library. Learn why that area was made a refuge. What plants and animals are especially protected there? What laws or park regulations protect the creatures that live there?

6. Is there any activity that takes place annually in your community and is considered a community tradition? How did that celebration or event begin? What events take place during the celebration? What do you like best about it? Is there any event that you are looking forward to taking part in when you are older?

7. The two children in *Misty of Chincoteague* have their hearts set on owning a particular horse. Have you ever had your heart set on owning an animal? What happened? How do you feel about the way things turned out?

8. The two children in the story work toward a goal for an entire year. What is the longest you have ever worked for a goal? Are you presently working toward a goal? What did you do or what are you doing to reach your goal?

9. Become familiar with the words about horses that appear in the Glossary on page three of this study guide. Knowing these words will help you understand the story.

PART I: CHAPTERS 1, 2

Vocabulary: Draw a line from each word on the left to its definition on the right. Then use the numbered words to fill in the blanks in the sentences below.

1. phantom	a. sailing ship of centuries ago
2. vexation	b. slightly salty
3. abide	c. ghost; creature that doesn't really exist
4. galleon	d. high underwater mound
5. shoal	e. endure; bear patiently
6. brackish	f. irritation; annoyance

. . . .

1. The stormy wind blew the __________________ toward the rocky island.
2. The ship hit a hidden __________________, causing its hull to be ripped open.
3. Had the boy seen a real, living horse or only a(n) __________________?
4. The horses drank from the __________________ pools beside the seashore.
5. "I can't __________________ seeing the colts separated from their mothers," said the young trainer.
6. With a look of __________________ on his face, the sea captain faced the darkening sky.

> Read to find out why there were wild horses on Assateague Island.

Questions:

1. Why was it crucial to keep the ponies alive aboard the *Santo Christo*?
2. How did the horses reach Assateague Island?
3. How did the ponies adapt to their new home?
4. Why was Assateague Island a particularly good environment for the horses?

Questions for Discussion:

1. How did the author make the background history of the horses seem as exciting as an adventure story?
2. Did you feel any sympathy for the men on the ship? Why or why not?

Part I: Chapters 1, 2 (cont.)

Literary Devices:

I. *Metaphor* — A metaphor is a suggested comparison between two unlike objects. For example:

> The sea became a wildcat now and the galleon her prey. She stalked the ship. . . . She slapped at her, rolling her victim from side to side.

What is being compared in this extended metaphor?

___

What is the effect of this comparison?

___

___

II. *Personification* — Personification in literature is a device in which an author grants human qualities to nonhman subjects. For example:

> The wildcat sea yawned, she swallowed the men.

What is being personified?

___

Why is this better than just saying, "The men fell into the sea and drowned."?

___

___

Literary Element: Setting

The setting of a work of literature refers to the time and place in which the story occurs. What is the setting of Chapters One and Two?

___

What clues indicate that the sequence of events described in these chapters took place in time past? About how long ago might this have been?

___

___

Writing Activity:

Imagine you were the ship's captain aboard the *Santo Christo*, and you were able to communicate your situation in order to obtain help. Write a message to send abroad that describes your predicament, your location, and your concerns.

PART II: CHAPTERS 3 - 5

Vocabulary: Many words have more than one meaning. Choose the definition that fits the way the underlined word is used in each of the sentences below. Write the letter of the definition you choose on the line to the right.

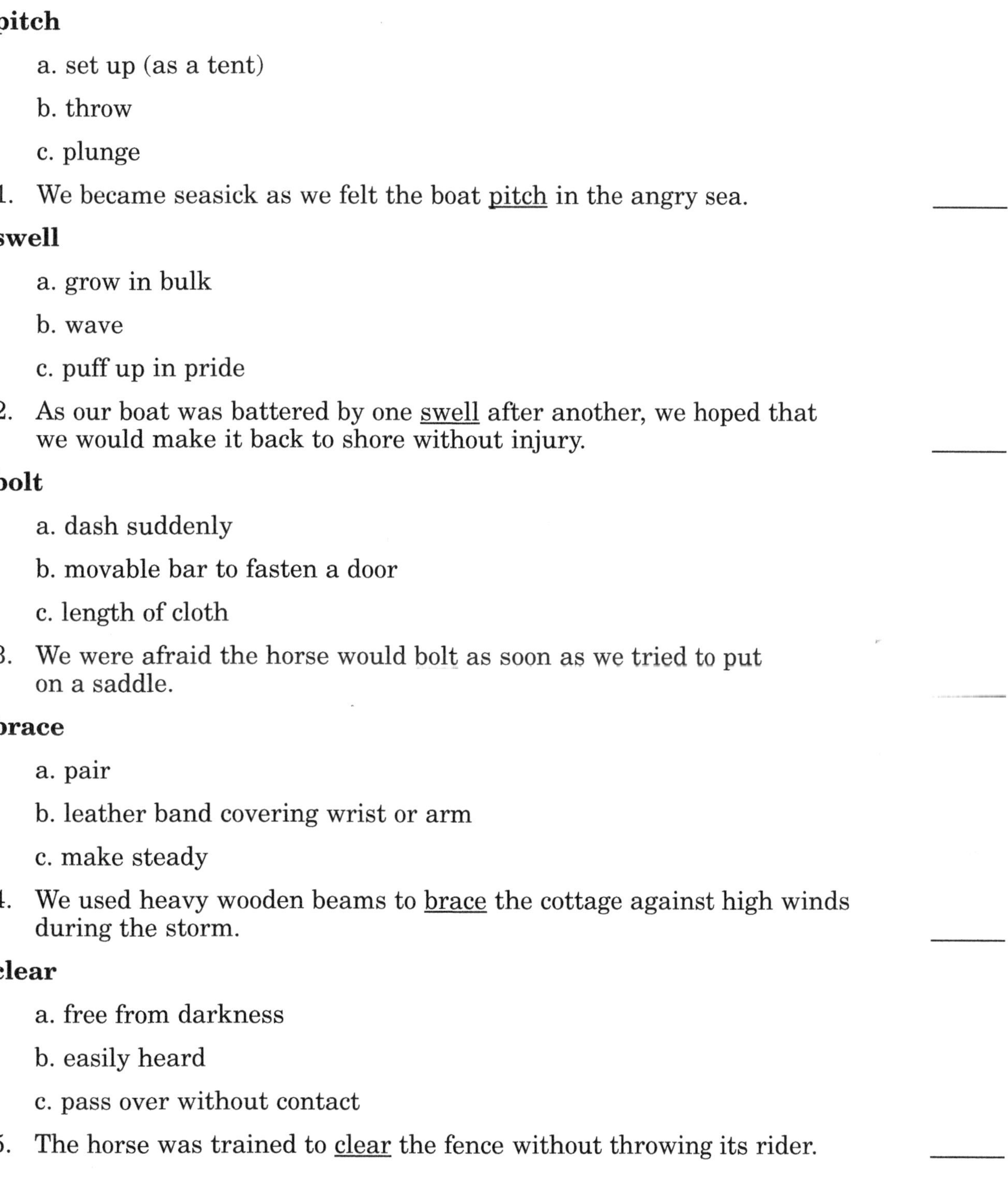

pitch

a. set up (as a tent)

b. throw

c. plunge

1. We became seasick as we felt the boat pitch in the angry sea. ______

swell

a. grow in bulk

b. wave

c. puff up in pride

2. As our boat was battered by one swell after another, we hoped that we would make it back to shore without injury. ______

bolt

a. dash suddenly

b. movable bar to fasten a door

c. length of cloth

3. We were afraid the horse would bolt as soon as we tried to put on a saddle. ______

brace

a. pair

b. leather band covering wrist or arm

c. make steady

4. We used heavy wooden beams to brace the cottage against high winds during the storm. ______

clear

a. free from darkness

b. easily heard

c. pass over without contact

5. The horse was trained to clear the fence without throwing its rider. ______

Part II: Chapters 3 - 5 (cont.)

Read to find out why Maureen and Paul looked forward to Pony Penning Day.

Questions:

1. Why did Maureen and Paul come to Assateague Island?
2. What made Maureen feel as though she was trespassing on Assateague Island?
3. Why were Maureen and Paul fascinated with the Phantom?
4. What plans did Maureen and Paul have for the Phantom?
5. Why did the natives of Chincoteague establish an annual Pony Penning Day?
6. How did Grandpa react when he heard about the children's plans for the Phantom?

Questions for Discussion:

1. Do you think Maureen and Paul set a realistic goal for themselves?
2. Do you think Grandpa should have been more supportive of the children's plans?

Literary Device: Personification

What is being personified in the following passage?

> Spring tides had come once more to Assateague Island. They were washing and salting the earth, coaxing new green spears to replace the old dried grasses.

___

What mood does this create?

___

___

Science Connection:

Do some research to learn about the sea creatures that inhabit the waters around Chincoteague and Assateague Islands. Include the following that were mentioned in the book:

- fiddler crabs
- clams
- oysters
- soft-shell crabs

Part II: Chapters 3 - 5 (cont.)

Cooking Activity:

You can have the same snack that Maureen and Paul ate in Grandma's kitchen. Here are recipes for cornbread and berry jam.

Corn Bread

What you need:

1 egg
1/2 cup apple juice concentrate
1/2 cup milk
1/4 cup vegetable oil
1 banana, mashed
1 cup all-purpose flour
1 tablespoon baking powder
1/2 teaspoon salt
1 cup yellow cornmeal

What you do:

1. Mix together the first five ingredients.
2. Stir together the rest of the ingredients in a separate bowl.
3. Stir together the wet and dry ingredients until just moist.
4. Pour mixture into a greased 8-inch baking pan.
5. Bake at 400° for 25 to 30 minutes.

Berry Jam

What you need:

1 cup strawberries hulled and cut in half
1/2 cup cranberries
1 1/2 cups blueberries
1 1/2 cups sugar

What you do:

1. Wash and dry the berries.
2. Stir the berries and the sugar together in a glass bowl.
3. Cook covered in the microwave for 10 minutes at full power.
4. Stir the mixture and cook 5 minutes more.
5. Cool the mixture, cover bowl, and refrigerate.

Writing Activity:

Write about a time when you set a challenging goal for yourself. Tell what you did to try to reach your goal, whether you received any help along the way, and whether you were successful.

PART II: CHAPTERS 6, 7

Vocabulary: Synonyms are words with similar meanings. Draw a line from each word in column A to its synonym in column B. Then use the words in column A to fill in the blanks in the sentences below.

A	B
1. taunted	a. turmoil
2. sultry	b. illusion
3. mirage	c. quiet
4. tension	d. torrid
5. subdued	e. ridiculed
6. commotion	f. anxiety

. . . .

1. A feeling of ___________________ overcame Paul as he saw the Phantom race toward the forest.
2. Even an ocean breeze could not cool them on a ___________________ August day.
3. Paul wondered whether he really saw the Phantom or if it was just a ___________________.
4. In the schoolyard, the older children shamelessly ___________________ the young ones, knowing they would not be punished.
5. The ___________________ of Pony Penning Day was in sharp contrast to the usual quiet atmosphere of Chincoteague Island.
6. The waves that had come crashing to shore were ___________________ now that the storm had passed.

Read to find out Paul discovers Misty.

Questions:

1. Why was Paul angry when he was sent after stragglers during the roundup? Why did he obey?
2. What did Paul discover when he went to retrieve the stragglers?
3. What difficult choice did Paul have to make?
4. How did the Phantom's colt get her name?

Part II: Chapters 6, 7 (cont.)

Questions for Discussion:

1. Do you think Paul should have captured the ponies?
2. How was Paul's first encounter with the Phantom different from what he had imagined?

Language Study: Dialect

The Beebe family speaks in the dialect of the Virginia coast. Rewrite each of the following sentences in standard English.

"It's nigh unto noontide, and your Grandma is having sixteen head to dinner tomorrow."

"Why, I heard tell 'twas the Indians chanced on 'em first."

Find another sentence in the story that contains dialect. Rewrite it below and then write it in standard English.

Literary Devices:

I. *Cliffhanger* — A cliffhanger is a device borrowed from early films in which an episode ended at the moment of greatest tension. In a book it is usually placed at the end of a chapter to encourage the reader to continue reading. What is the cliffhanger at the end of Chapter Seven?

Part II: Chapters 6, 7 (cont.)

II. *Point of View* — Point of view in literature refers to the voice telling the story. One of the characters may tell the story, or the author may tell the story.

From whose point of view is this story told?

____

Why do you think the author chose this point of view?

____

____

____

Writing Activity:

Imagine you are a reporter from a Baltimore newspaper who has been sent to Chincoteague Island for Pony Penning Day. Write a newspaper article describing what has happened so far.

PART II: CHAPTERS 8, 9

Vocabulary: Antonyms are words with opposite meanings. Draw a line from each word in column A to its antonym in column B. Then use the words in column A to fill in the blanks in the sentences below.

	A		B
1.	murmur	a.	flows
2.	ebbs	b.	level
3.	nimble	c.	overweight
4.	steep	d.	awkward
5.	slender	e.	sad
6.	ecstasy	f.	bellow
7.	contented	g.	depression

. . . .

1. A feeling of __________________ came over Maureen when she realized that the Phantom, a horse she adored, might soon be her own.
2. Walking up the __________________ river bank made our legs feel strained and painful.
3. We can walk on the beach once more when the tide __________________.
4. Paul felt __________________ once the horses and their colts were safely ashore.
5. Everyone admired the Phantom's arched neck and well-proportioned __________________ body.
6. A(n) __________________ of delight swept through the crowd as it watched the magnificent horses walk through town.
7. With each moment that passed after it was born, the colt became less tottery and more and more __________________.

Read to learn about Paul's plan for Phantom and Misty.

Questions:

1. How did the colt manage to get across the water from Assateague to Chincoteague Island?
2. How did the Phantom protect Misty from the stampede of horses coming ashore?
3. How did Grandpa feel about Paul's activities on Pony Penning Day?
4. Why did the colt seem happier than the rest of the herd in Chincoteague?
5. How did Paul plan to buy both the Phantom and Misty?

Part II: Chapters 8, 9 (cont.)

Questions for Discussion:

1. How do you think Grandpa really felt about Paul and Maureen buying the Phantom and Misty?
2. Do you think the fire chief will go along with Paul's plan to buy the Phantom and Misty?

Literary Device: Simile

A simile is a comparison of two unlike objects using the words "like" and "as." For example:

Grandpa's voice was as strong as a tow rope.

What is being compared?

____

Why is this better than just saying, "Grandpa had a strong voice."?

____

____

Writing Activity:

Continue the article you began as a reporter for a Baltimore newspaper. Describe the horses crossing the bay and Paul's rescue of Misty. Include some statements that you might have gotten from townspeople who viewed the horses as they walked through town.

PART II: CHAPTERS 10 - 12

Vocabulary: Draw a line from each word on the left to its definition on the right. Then use the numbered words to fill in the blanks in the sentences below.

1. torrents	a. funny actions; capers
2. frisking	b. make a surprise attack from a hidden place
3. antics	c. take care of; meet the needs of
4. competitor	d. moving in a lively way
5. fend	e. violent streams of water
6. ambush	f. rival; one who tries to win something that others want

. . . .

1. As the high-spirited colt was ________________ in the corral, it seemed as if it were dancing.

2. When the colts stopped drinking their mothers' milk, they were old enough to ________________ for themselves.

3. The horsemen tried to ________________ the wild pony by waiting patiently in the woods until it came near.

4. During the storm, ________________ of rain poured over the eaves of the roof.

5. The children laughed at the ________________ of the young colt as it kicked up its heels and ran round and round in circles.

6. The winning racehorse beat his fastest ________________ by two yards.

Read to find out why Phantom began to trust Paul.

Questions:

1. How did Maureen and Paul react when they saw the penned-up colts? What did they decide to do?
2. Why didn't the outcome of the evening race surprise the spectators? What decision did this lead Paul to make about next year's race? Do you think this is realistic?
3. Why did the fire chief sell Misty? How did he feel about this?
4. Why did the Phantom begin to trust Paul?

Part II: Chapters 10 - 12 (cont.)

Questions for Discussion:

1. Why do you think Maureen and Paul had their hearts set on owning the Phantom and Misty? Do you think that they had good reasons for wanting these ponies rather than any others? Were they justified in being miserable because they weren't able to get what they wanted? How would you have reacted in the same situation?
2. Imagine that you are Grandpa Beebe. What advice would you give the children?
3. Do you think Maureen and Paul could have prevented Misty's sale?

Science Connection:

Do some research to find out how a horse changes and grows during its first two years of life. What skills are the most important ones it develops? When does it become able to fend for itself?

Literary Device: Cliffhanger

What is the cliffhanger at the end of Chapter Twelve? What do you think might happen next?

___

___

___

Writing Activity:

Have you ever had a disappointment similar to the one that Paul and Maureen experienced in Chapter Twelve? Draw on what you learned from your own experience to write the two children a sympathetic letter. Give them advice that you think might comfort them.

PART II: CHAPTERS 13 - 15

Vocabulary: Use the context to figure out the meaning of the underlined words in each of the sentences below. Circle the letter of the word you choose.

1. The children stared <u>fixedly</u> at the colts as if memorizing every detail of their bodies.
   a. sleepily b. steadily c. crankily d. distractedly
2. The horse <u>tolerated</u> the rider for only a few seconds before it threw him off.
   a. endured b. rejected c. gentled d. nuzzled
3. Once the pony's legs were <u>splayed</u>, the children were able to brush its mane.
   a. spotted b. slender c. injured d. spread
4. The <u>vicious</u> horseflies swarmed all over the horses, stinging them again and again.
   a. fierce b. vivid c. lazy d. gentle
5. When flies would <u>light</u> on the mare, she tried to brush them off with a swish of her tail.
   a. die b. explode c. land d. illuminate
6. With a burst of energy, the horse began to <u>surge</u> ahead of the other riders.
   a. rush b. plod c. wander d. canter
7. Although Paul loved the pot pie, his appetite was so <u>puny</u> that he could hardly finish a little portion.
   a. great b. small c. eclectic d. exotic

Read to find out why Maureen and Paul were training Phantom.

Questions:

1. How did Maureen and Paul's disappointment affect them for the rest of the week?
2. What happened to make the children's dream come true?
3. How was Misty different from other colts that the children had known?
4. How did the children train the Phantom to accept a rider? How did their grand-father feel about this unusual method of training?
5. What was the purpose of the fire chief's call? Why was the Beebe family amused by his visit?
6. What did the people of Chincoteague think about the Phantom's chance of beating Black Comet in the race?

Part II: Chapters 13 - 15 (cont.)

Questions for Discussion:

1. What do you think the Phantom's fate should be?
2. When Maureen hugged the boy who gave up Misty, Paul told the boy not to mind her because her behavior was "just girl's fribble." Earlier in the story, Paul told Maureen to quit acting like a girl. What do you think of Paul's attitude toward his sister and toward girls? What would you say to him about it?

Literary Technique: Descriptive Language

Through the use of descriptive words, an author can help readers visualize what is happening. Read the following passage from *Misty of Chincoteague* and then underline the words and phrases that help you "see" the running horse.

> The Phantom was wild with happiness when she raced. She showed it in the arching of her neck, in the upward pluming of her tail, in the flaring of her nostrils. Paul or Maureen had only to close their legs in on her sides to make her surge forward. Then she would skim the earth like the gulls she knew so well.

Art Connection:

Create a poster inviting mainlanders to come to Chincoteague for the events of Pony Penning Day and auction day. Describe some of the highlights of the celebration and illustrate your poster.

Writing Activities:

1. Imagine that you live on Chincoteague. Write a letter inviting a friend to come to stay with you during Pony Penning Day and the day after. Describe some of the things you might do together.
2. Imagine that you are Grandma or Grandpa Beebe. Write a journal entry about your activities on the days after Pony Penning Day. Tell your thoughts and worries about Paul and Maureen.

PART II: CHAPTERS 16 - 18

Vocabulary: Use the words from the Word Box and the clues below to complete the crossword puzzle.

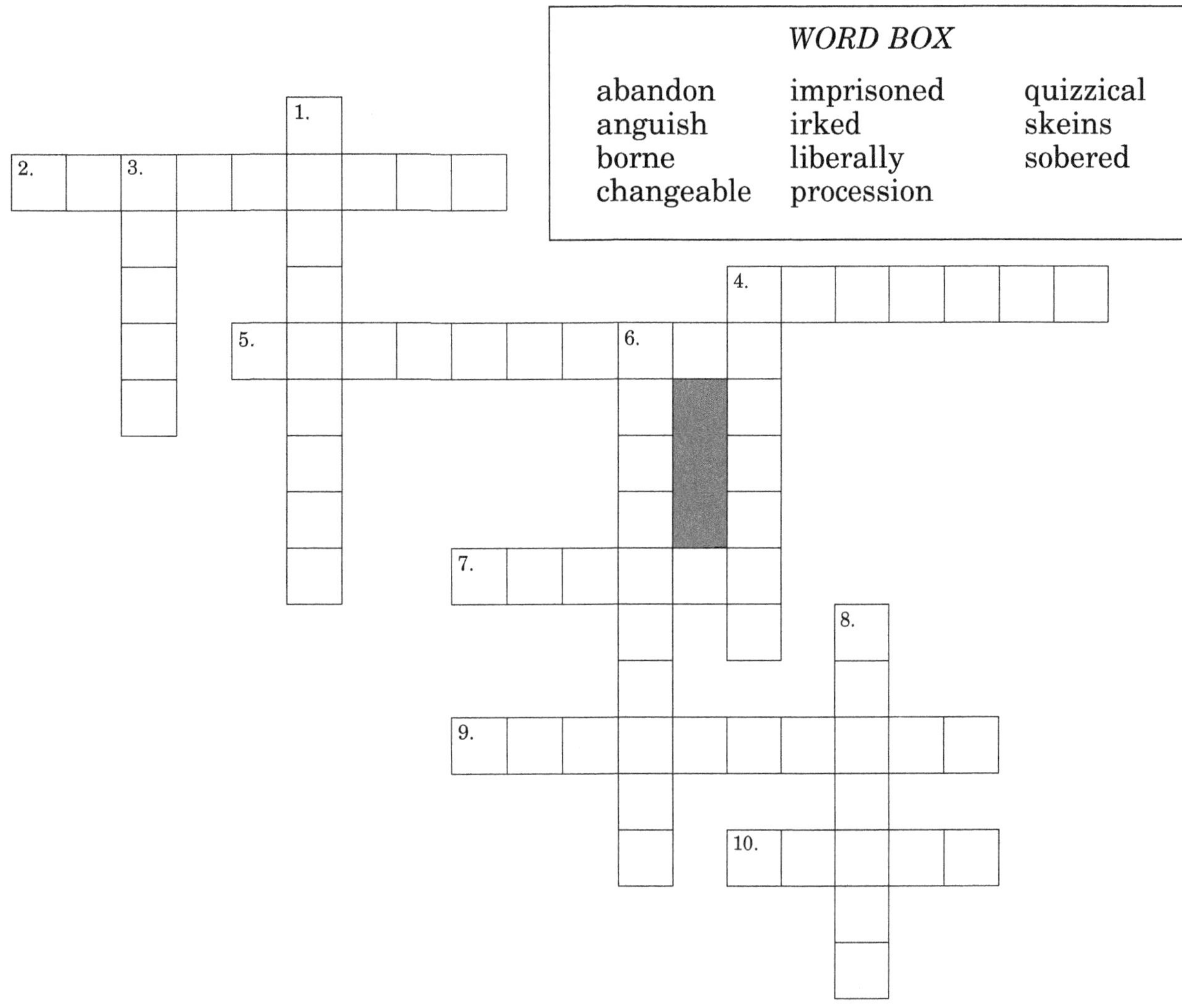

Across

2. questioning; puzzled
4. complete freedom
5. line or body of persons moving along in orderly succession
7. loose bundles of yarn
9. quick to say, think, or do something quite different
10. carried

Down

1. generously
3. annoyed
4. misery
6. made someone or something a captive
8. became serious

Part II: Chapters 16 - 18 (cont.)

Read to find out which horse won the race on Pony Penning Day.

Questions:

1. What caused tension between Maureen and Paul before the race? How was the issue settled? Do you think this was a fair way to reach a decision?
2. Why were the crowds greater than usual at this year's Pony Penning Day?
3. Why did Maureen sit by herself to watch the race?
4. How did Black Comet's attitude before the race differ from the Phantom's attitude? Why did Maureen think the Phantom won?
5. How comfortable did the Phantom become with life on Chincoteague? What event called her back to Assateague?
6. What choices did the children have when the Phantom was tempted to return to Assateague? Why do you think Paul gave the Phantom her freedom?
7. Why was Misty left behind on Chincoteague Island?

Questions for Discussion:

1. Do you think Paul should have given the Phantom her freedom?
2. Do you think Misty will be as swift a racehorse as her mother?
3. Has reading this book given you any insights into the world of wild things? Has it changed or made you take a closer look at any of your attitudes?

Literary Devices: Simile and Metaphor

Underline the simile or metaphor in each of the sentences below. Then write "S" for simile or "M" for metaphor on the line to the right.

1. The sun was a huge red balloon hovering over the bay . . . ______
2. . . . a light wind came up, whisking sheep clouds before it. ______
3. . . . she [Phantom] was caught like a fly in a web. ______
4. When they [the crowd] discovered Maureen standing on the top rail of the fence like a bird on a twig, friends and strangers cheered. ______

Part II: Chapters 16 - 18 (cont.)

Literary Element: Plot

The plot of a novel is the planned series of events that occur during the course of the book. Often authors present a series of problems to be solved. To keep readers reading, they may follow each solution with a new problem. The chart below shows some problems that occur in *Misty of Chincoteague*. Complete the chart by writing the solution to each problem.

Problem	Solution
Maureen and Paul needed money to buy the Phantom.	
The Phantom was so wild it could not be captured in earlier roundups.	
The children had trouble getting enough money to buy both the Phantom and Misty.	
The Phantom and Misty were sold to someone else.	
The children wanted the Phantom to win the race against Black Comet.	
The Phantom seemed unhappy.	

Writing Activities:

Did you ever give up something you wanted to have or do in order to make another person happy? Write about your experience. Tell *what* you gave up and *why* you gave it up. Tell how you felt about your decision.

CLOZE ACTIVITY

The following passage has been taken from Chapter Seven. Read it through completely. Then go back and fill in each blank with one word that makes sense. Afterwards, you may compare your language with that of the author.

Tom's Point was a protected piece of land where the marsh was hard and the grass especially sweet. About seventy wild ponies, ____________[1] by their morning's run, stood browsing quietly, ____________[2] if they were in a corral. Only ____________[3] they looked up at their captors. The ____________[4] meadow and their own weariness kept them ____________[5] prisoners.

At a watchful distance the roundup ____________[6] rested their mounts and relaxed. It was ____________[7] the lull in the midst of a ____________.[8] All was quiet on the surface. Yet ____________[9] was an undercurrent of tension. You could ____________[10] it in the narrowed eyes of the ____________,[11] their subdued voices and their too easy ____________.[12]

Suddenly the laughter stilled. Mouths gaped in ____________.[13] Eyes rounded. For a few seconds no ____________[14] spoke at all. Then a shout that ____________[15] half wonder and half admiration went up ____________[16] the men. Paul Beebe was bringing in *the* ____________[17] *and a colt*!

Even the wild herds ____________[18] excited. As one horse, they stopped grazing. ____________[19] head jerked high, to see and to ____________[20] the newcomers. The Pied Piper whirled out and ____________[21] the mare and her colt into his ____________.[22] He sniffed them all over as if ____________[23] make sure that nothing had harmed them. ____________[24] he snorted at Phantom, as much as ____________[25] say, "You cause me more trouble than ____________[26] the rest of my mares put together!"

____________[27] roundup men were swarming around Paul, buzzing ____________[28] questions.

"How'd you *do* it, Paul?" Wyle Maddox ____________[29] over the excited hubbub.

"Where'd you find 'em?" ____________[30] Kim Horsepepper.

Paul made no answer. The questions floated around and above him like voices in a dream.

POST-READING ACTIVITIES

1. Return to the K-W-L chart that you began in the Pre-Reading Activities on page four of this study guide. Correct any misconceptions you had about horses and add any information you gained from reading this book.
2. **Cooperative Learning Activity:** Work with a small group of your classmates to discuss your attitudes toward wild animals. Is it all right to keep wild animals as personal pets or put them into zoos? How do you feel about animals such as monkeys, elephants, and horses being trained to work for people? What should society do when animal populations get so large that the animals begin to have difficulty surviving, when wild animals menace campers or people living in rural areas, and when wild animals cause problems for farmers? Try to reach a consensus within your group and then compare your conclusions with those of other groups.
3. **Cooperative Learning Activity:** With a small group of your classmates, create a mural-map that shows the events of Pony Penning Day. Some sites to include might be Assateague Island, the channel, the main street of Chincoteague, the pony pens, and the Beebes' ranch.
4. **Pair / Share:** *Misty of Chincoteague* was published in 1947. Which of the story events do you think could take place today? Which do you think are unlikely to take place today? Discuss these questions with a reading partner.
5. Write a description of your own community, in which you compare and contrast it with Chincoteague. Are there any ways in which your community is similar? In what ways is it different? Tell why you prefer your own community to Chincoteague, or tell why you wish it were more like Chincoteague.
6. With a partner or small group of classmates, improvise a scene that wasn't in the story but might have been. For example:
   - Paul and Maureen talk about their plans as they work together to earn money to buy the Phantom.
   - Grandpa tries to comfort the two children after they learn that Misty and the Phantom have been sold.
   - At the racetrack, Maureen's friends try to comfort her for not being the one to ride in the race.
   - Paul and Maureen tell their friends why they let the Phantom go free.
7. Just when the children think they have lost Misty and the Phantom, they are given a chance to buy them. How much do you think this story event is like something that could happen in real life? If you were to change the story to make it as much like your idea of real life as possible, what changes would you make?
8. In a group, take turns telling one another about your goals. Then brainstorm to make a list of things that each person might do to achieve his or her goal. Record the ideas that can help you realize your own goal.
9. On your own or with a partner, create a "photo album" for the first year that Paul and Maureen cared for Misty and Phantom. Draw pictures that show the children's experiences caring for the horses and gentling the Phantom. Write a caption for each picture. You might choose to write from the point of view of Maureen or Paul.

SUGGESTIONS FOR FURTHER READING

Fiction

* Armstrong, William H. *Sounder*. HarperCollins.
Bryant, Bonnie. *Horse Crazy*. Yearling.
Clifford, Eth. *The Summer of the Dancing Horse*. Author House.
Doty, Jean Slaughter. *The Valley of the Ponies*. Simon & Schuster.
__________________. *Yesterday's Horses*. Atheneum.
Dunn, Marylois. *The Absolutely Perfect Horse*. HarperCollins.
* Gardiner, John Reynolds. *Stone Fox*. HarperCollins.
* Gipson, Fred. *Old Yeller*. HarperCollins.
Highlights Editors. *Storm's Fury and Other Horse Stories*. Boyd's Mills Press.
Morey, Walt. *Runaway Stallion*. Blue Heron.
* Naylor, Phyllis Reynolds. *Shiloh*. Atheneum.
Peck, Robert Newton. *Soup in the Saddle*. Yearling.
* Rawlings, Marjorie Kinnan. *The Yearling*. Aladdin.
* Rawls, Wilson. *Where the Red Fern Grows*. Yearling
Rounds, Glen. *Wild Appaloosa*. Holiday House.
Sewell, Anna. *Black Beauty*. Dover.
Springer, Nancy. *A Horse to Love*. HarperCollins.
* Steinbeck, John. *The Red Pony*. Penguin.
Szymanski, Lois. *Chincoteague Ponies: Untold Tails*. Schiffer Publishing.
Towne, Mary. *Boxed In*. HarperCollins.
Tripp, Valerie. *Meet Felicity*. Pleasant Company.
* White, E.B. *Charlotte's Web*. HarperCollins.

Nonfiction

Jauck, Andrea and Points, Larry. *Assateague: Island of Wild Ponies*. Sierra Press.

Some Other Books by Marguerite Henry

Album of Horses. Aladdin.
Black Gold. Aladdin.
Born to Trot. Aladdin.
Brighty of the Grand Canyon. Aladdin.
Justin Morgan Had a Horse. Aladdin.
King of the Wind. Aladdin.
Misty's Twilight. Aladdin.
Mustang, Wild Spirit of the West. Aladdin.
A Pictorial Life Story of Misty. Aladdin.
Sea Star, Orphan of Chincoteague. Aladdin.
Stormy: Misty's Foal. Aladdin.
White Stallion of Lipizza. Aladdin.

* NOVEL-TIES Study Guides are available for these titles.

ANSWER KEY

Part I
Chapters 1, 2

Vocabulary: 1. c 2. f 3. e 4. a 5. d 6. b; 1. galleon 2. shoal 3. phantom 4. brackish 5. abide 6. vexation

Questions: 1. It was crucial to keep the ponies alive until the galleon reached Puerto Bello, where they were to be delivered to the Viceroy of Peru in exchange for gold. 2. A great storm sank the ship and washed the ponies ashore on Assateague Island. 3. The ponies adapted to the island by learning how to find food and water, how to plunge in the sea to protect themselves from insect pests, and how to get out of mud holes. They grew shaggy coats to keep themselves warm. 4. Assateague Island was an excellent environment for the horses because there was an ample supply of salt grass and myrtle to eat, water to drink, and a mild climate. There were no natural predators.

Part II
Chapters 3 - 5

Vocabulary: 1. c 2. b 3. a 4. c 5. c

Questions: 1. Maureen and Paul came to Assateague Island with their grandfather, who had brought the game warden to see how the animals weathered the winter. 2. On Assateague Island, Maureen thought she was trespassing on a ship's graveyard — the ship that had been wrecked in an earlier century. 3. So many legends had grown up about the horse that couldn't be captured that Maureen and Paul were intrigued. Not even certain that the Phantom really existed, they wanted to own this mysterious animal. 4. Maureen and Paul planned to save their money from working on Grandpa's horse farm and doing other odd jobs around the bay in order to buy the Phantom when she was captured on Pony Penning Day. 5. The first Pony Penning Day was established solely for sport, but it came to be a necessary annual event to thin the herd. The money raised from the sale of the horses was used to support the local fire department. 6. When Grandpa first heard the children's plans, he began to laugh at them for believing the Phantom could be theirs. When he realized they were serious, he tried to discourage them from a futile effort.

Chapters 6, 7

Vocabulary: 1. e 2. d 3. b 4. f 5. c 6. a; 1. tension 2. sultry 3. mirage 4. taunted 5. commotion 6. subdued

Questions: 1. Paul was angry because he felt he was being sent out of the way to get rid of him. He obeyed because he had promised his grandfather that he would do as his leader told him. 2. When Paul went to retrieve the stragglers, he discovered the Phantom alone with a brand new colt. 3. Paul had to decide whether to let the Phantom and her colt go free or try to bring them in. Although he knew the ponies loved their independence, he wanted to own them so much that he decided to try to round them up. 4. When Paul first saw the colt, he had seen a silver flash that looked like mist with the sun on it. When he spoke aloud of her, he found himself calling her Misty.

Chapters 8, 9

Vocabulary: 1. f 2. a 3. d 4. b 5. c 6. g 7. e; 1. ecstasy 2. steep 3. ebbs 4. contented 5. slender 6. murmur 7. nimble

Questions: 1. To get from Assateague to Chincoteague Island, Phantom pushed her colt into the water and Paul jumped into the water to guide the colt when it was running into trouble. 2. The Phantom used her own body to protect the colt by straddling it as the horses came ashore. 3. Grandpa was very proud of Paul for capturing the Phantom and helping the colt come ashore. He also seemed proud that Paul acted in a mature, courageous manner. 4. All the horses except Misty were confused and fatigued. Misty seemed content just to be near her mother and be well fed. 5. Paul planned to offer the fire chief the hundred dollars he and Maureen had earned to pay for the Phantom with the promise that another sum of money would be forthcoming for Misty.

Chapters 10 - 12

Vocabulary: 1. e 2. d 3. a 4. f 5. c 6. b; 1. frisking 2. fend 3. ambush 4. torrents 5. antics 6. competitor

Questions: 1. Paul and Maureen were upset because the penned-up colts seemed lost, scared, and hungry. They asked the fire chief if they could feed the hungry colts but were told that the colts were old enough to fend for themselves and that separating them from their mothers was the kindest way to start them taking care of themselves. 2. It was no surprise that Black Comet won the race because he had done so for the last three years and had no serious competition. Paul decided that the Phantom would win the next year's race. Answers to the last part of the question will vary. 3. The fire chief sold Misty because he had never heard Paul's words when he explained his plan to pay for the Phantom and her colt. He was apologetic for selling Misty. 4. When Paul went in search of Misty because a storm had burst, he found the colt and its mother sheltered in his grandfather's truck. He spent the night comforting them. Subsequently, the Phantom lost some of her distrust of him.

Chapters 13 - 15

Vocabulary: 1. b 2. a 3. d 4. a 5. c 6. a 7. b

Questions: 1. For the rest of the week, the children felt as if they no longer belonged to the happy crowds, and although they tried to carry on as usual, they seemed to be living in a dream. They blamed themselves for having let the ponies be sold to someone else. 2. The man who had purchased Misty discovered that he had won another colt in a raffle. Because his son preferred the other colt, the man was delighted to be given the chance to back out of the sale. The sheriff then sold Misty and the Phantom to Paul and Maureen. 3. Unlike other colts who gradually learned from their mothers to trust humans, Misty was accepting of humans and curious about them long before her mother. She enjoyed their attention from the start. 4. The children tied a small sack of sand to the Phantom's back to accustom her to the idea of a rider. When they rode her, they rode bareback and used only a rope instead of a regular saddle, bit, and bridle. Grandpa was proud of Maureen and Paul for gentling the Phantom and said that the standard riding gear was unnecessary. 5. The fire chief came to ask Paul and Maureen to enter the Phantom in the race on Pony Penning Day. The family was amused because they had taken it for granted that their horse would be in the race. 6. Some people felt that the Phantom was fast enough to beat Black Comet; others felt that she was too wild and undependable to race and that she might end up jumping the fence.

Chapters 16 - 18

Vocabulary: Across — 2. quizzical 4. abandon 5. procession 7. skeins 9. changeable 10. borne; Down — 1. liberally 3. irked 4. anguish 6. imprisoned 8. sobered

Questions: 1. Tension arose because Maureen and Paul did not know how to settle the question of who would ride the Phantom in the race. Grandpa had them settle the issue on a pulley bone (wish bone) and Paul won. Answers to the last part of the question will vary. 2. The crowd was larger this year as compared to prior years because everyone wanted to see the Phantom challenge Black Comet, the winner for the past three years. 3. Maureen decided to be by herself to watch the race, not wanting to experience the pity her family and friends would offer her because she was not racing the Phantom. Also, by sitting alone she could fantasize that she was both Paul and the Phantom. 4. Before the race, Black Comet seemed so calm as to be bored. The Phantom, on the other hand, was high-strung and impatient. Maureen thought the Phantom won because she raced for the sheer joy of it. This transported her beyond the other two horses. 5. The Phantom was not content living on Chincoteague for her spirit seemed to be somewhere far away from her body. The morning after the race, as the children were giving the Phantom a run on the beach, the Pied Piper swam across the channel to bring the Phantom back to the island. 6. The children could have driven the mare back into the corral or let it go. Paul chose to give the Phantom her freedom. Answers to the second part of the question will vary, but should include the idea that Paul realized that the Phantom's spirit was on the island with the other wild things. 7. Misty was left behind because she was old enough to fend for herself. She belonged on Chincoteague because she was happy living among people.